THE MOON OF THE
CHICKAREES

THE THIRTEEN MOONS

The Moon of the Owls (JANUARY)

The Moon of the Bears (FEBRUARY)

The Moon of the Salamanders (MARCH)

The Moon of the Chickarees (APRIL)

The Moon of the Monarch Butterflies (MAY)

The Moon of the Fox Pups (JUNE)

The Moon of the Wild Pigs (JULY)

The Moon of the Mountain Lions (AUGUST)

The Moon of the Deer (SEPTEMBER)

The Moon of the Alligators (OCTOBER)

The Moon of the Gray Wolves (NOVEMBER)

The Moon of the Winter Bird (DECEMBER)

The Moon of the Moles (DECEMBER-JANUARY)

NEW EDITION   THE THIRTEEN MOONS

THE MOON OF THE
CHICKAREES

BY JEAN CRAIGHEAD GEORGE

ILLUSTRATED BY DON RODELL

HarperCollins*Publishers*

The Moon of the Chickarees
Text copyright © 1969, 1992 by Jean Craighead George
Illustrations copyright © 1992 by Don Rodell

Typography by Al Cetta
1   2   3   4   5   6   7   8   9   10
NEW EDITION

Library of Congress Cataloging-in-Publication Data
George, Jean Craighead, date
   The moon of the chickarees / by Jean Craighead George ;
illustrated by Don Rodell. — New ed.
      p.   cm. — (The Thirteen moons)
   Summary: Describes the activities of a mother red squirrel
during the month of April as she nurtures her newborn babies in
the Bitterroot Valley of Montana.
   ISBN 0-06-022507-6. — ISBN 0-06-022508-4 (lib. bdg.)
   1. Squirrels—Juvenile literature.   2. Tamiasciurus hudsonicus—
Montana—Bitterroot River Valley—Juvenile literature.
[1. Squirrels.]
I. Rodell, Don, ill.   II. Title.   III. Series: George, Jean
Craighead, date, Thirteen moons (HarperCollins)
QL795.S7G46   1992
599.32′32—dc20
                                                        90-22409
                                                        CIP
                                                        AC

Why is this series called The Thirteen Moons?

Each year there are either thirteen full moons or thirteen new moons. This series of books is named in their honor.

Our culture, which bases its calendar on sun-time, has no names for the thirteen moons. I have named the thirteen lunar months after thirteen North American animals. Primarily night prowlers, these animals, at a particular time of the year in a particular place, do wondrous things. The places are known to you, but the animal moon names are not, because I made them up. So that you can place them on our sun calendar, I have identified them with the names of our months. When I ran out of these, I gave the thirteenth moon, the Moon of the Moles, the expandable name December-January.

Fortunately, the animals do not need calendars, for names or no names, sun-time or moon-time, they follow their own inner clocks.

—Jean Craighead George

THE SUN AROSE. The sky turned yellow. The faintest hint of green showed on the April land. A furry face appeared in the hollow of a fir tree. *"TCHER - r - r - r - r - r - r - rrrrr, TCHERRR - r - r - r - r - r - r!"* The screamer's breath turned to ice stars in the cold air.

She was an American red squirrel, about eleven inches long with rusty-brown fur and short tufts on her ears. She sported a bushy tail that was fringed with silver hairs. Her jet-black eyes were outlined in white.

She was mad. Her rights were being violated.

From the southern tip of the Appalachian Mountains to the coniferous forests of the West, and northward through Canada and Alaska, the red squirrels make their homes. They are the chatterboxes of the forests, screaming at bears, jays, magpies, woodpeckers, gray squirrels, house cats—an endless list—skunks, lynxes, and particularly each other. They are called "boomers" in the South and East, "bummers" on the Pacific Coast, and "chickarees" in New England and the West. Their loudest and most frantic noises are directed at the birds and beasts who would steal food from their storehouses, which are piles of green spruce and pine cones.

"TCHERrrrrrrrrrrrrr!" The chickaree in the hollow was screaming at the gray jaybird who was taking the berries she had dried and stored last summer under the bark of a tree. He paid her no heed.

"TCHER-RRRRRRRRR," she screamed louder. He spread his smoky gray wings,

swallowed a berry, and chased a newly emerged beetle.

She protested again, then washed her face, brushed her ears, and looked down fourteen feet onto her small domain in the forest. It was only seventy feet across and sixty feet in length, but it was home and food and shelter—everything she needed for survival. It must be defended. The moon of April was rising, the moon of the rights of property owners.

"*TCHER-r-r-r,*" she called. She meant, "Get off my property!"

The chickaree's land lay along the Bitterroot River in Montana. Streams flowed into it from the Clearwater Mountains on the west and the Sapphire Mountains on the east. One of the streams, overflowing with snow melt this morning, cascaded through her property and spilled into the Bitterroot River. It made a gravel bar and a marsh where a huge moose browsed.

The chickaree screamed. Her cousin, and also

her neighbor, was sneaking through last year's dried cow parsnips along the stream, to the tree where she stored her toadstools and mushrooms. Last autumn she had laid them out on a log, and when they were dry, she had hidden them under the bark of a limb on the old western hemlock.

Now they were about to be stolen, and she could do nothing about it. It was the first week in April, and she had just given birth to four babies, tiny, blind, and hairless. She could not leave them to chase her cousin. He picked up a mushroom, sat up, and stuffed it into one of his cheek pouches. Then he picked up another.

"TCHER-KERrrrr!" she exploded. So earsplitting was her cry that she startled the magpie in the river thicket nearby. The magpie, a large black bird with white belly and shoulders and a long iridescent green tail, had returned to the Bitterroot after wandering east to Wisconsin for the winter. He was almost as talkative and noisy as the chickaree.

In a very loud voice he yakked, and flew after a trespassing magpie. It was the moon of property owners, and the magpie was asserting his rights.

The chickaree had her own trespasser. Once more she scolded her cousin, this time so fiercely that he jumped from the hemlock and landed on her favorite boulder. She screamed again. Flicking his elegant tail, he ran home.

She went back to her babies and pulled them into her belly fur. Gently she held them against the April cold. The frost had bitten the Bitterroot valley last night. It had also nipped the sprouting blades of winter grain as far south as Kansas and the buds of the cherry blossoms in faraway Michigan.

The chickaree knew nothing of these things. She knew only that her babies must be nurtured.

As the hours passed, the day warmed to a pleasant 40 degrees Fahrenheit, but the little squirrel was unaware of it; she was only aware of her suckling young. Their eyes were closed, and their tails and legs were so short that they did not even vaguely resemble their acrobatic father. The chickaree had mated with him early in March when the snow was falling softly. Now, forty days later, she was tending their babies, just as her mother had tended her a year ago. The chickaree did not remember her mother's tongue or her gentle paws. She did not remember being rolled on her back, tipped on her side, and bitten softly, although she was doing this to her babies. Vague memories and an inherited code of red squirrel behavior guided her in motherhood.

Like her own babies, she had nursed and slept on her first day of life. Ten days later, she was furry with velvety fuzz. In twenty-seven days, her eyes and ears opened. She was weaned in five weeks. Just before that day she and her brothers and sisters ventured out of the den. They clung to the limbs of their home tree and practiced running and balancing. After several days they could jump from limb to limb. Grasping small twigs, they

swung and bounced in the sun-speckled shade. They went down to the ground on sunny days and, on rainy days, hid under logs. One day the chickaree and her siblings followed their mother to her huge three-foot-high storehouses of cones. Her excitement and her chittering conveyed to her youngsters the importance of storing food.

At the end of July the chickaree left home. She scurried down the mountain running along the limbs of one forest tree to the next. Occasionally she scurried over the ground. Ravens chased her, hawks pursued her, and other chickarees screamed at her when she crossed their property. Finally she arrived on this small patch of land on the shores of the Bitterroot River. She climbed the big hemlock. No red squirrels chased or screamed at her. She had found a home. It was a good home, rich with cone-bearing trees: Douglas firs, hemlocks, lodgepole pines, and a white spruce.

Immediately, she built herself hideouts. They

were nests of sticks and leaves in which to hide when the pine martens, her deadly enemies, were hunting her. She ate flower and grass seeds, cones, berries, mushrooms, insects, and sometimes bird eggs. She laid out highways through the trees, and she chittered and screeched constantly. When she had built safe places to hide, she started her storehouse.

When the spruce cones were large and green and the lodgepole pine cones were ripe, she was a busy chickaree. She ran to every part of her property, including the highest treetops and the forest floor. She sat on stumps peeling cones and eating the seeds. The leftovers she put in her storehouse. She worked all day long and even in the moonlight when the owls were hunting.

She cut and dropped green cones to the ground, then put them in the water so they would not dry out and shed their seeds. Mushrooms and toadstools she laid in the sun to dry. She buried berries in pine needles to preserve them, and all the while she chittered and clucked.

While she worked, she scolded the jays, the pack rats, the mice, the woodpeckers, and the nuthatches—all the creatures that came to steal from her storehouse.

And she screeched most ferociously at the marten who included her property in his own home range of seven square miles. He did not want her food; he wanted her.

In November her cousin moved into the half acre right next to hers, and she devoted much of her time to scolding him. His land was not as rich as hers, and he would sneak over their border and steal from her storehouse. Some foods she buried in the ground to protect them from this marauder.

When the cold winds howled and the leaves blew off the willows and cottonwoods along the river, the chickaree built herself a winter nest in the dense foliage at the top of a Douglas fir. She made it both windproof and rainproof with leaves, pine needles, moss, and dry twigs.

Cleverly designed, it was about twenty inches wide and several feet deep. The room inside was lined with insulating rootlets and soft plant fibers. During December and January, when the snow locked up the valley of the Bitterroot, she spent much of her time sleeping in her cozy winter home—unless a trespasser came on her land—and then she was awake and chittering. Toward the end of February she stopped screaming and took a mate.

When the white starflowers opened and the fragrant balsamroot flowered in the first week in April, she left her winter home and her mate and moved into the black-backed woodpecker's abandoned home in a big Douglas fir tree. She lined the cavity with fibers and soft needles. Then, as the early birds arrived from South America and the fish snapped miller moths off the surface of the river, she gave birth.

Unlike the chickaree, some property owners shared. Across the river in the grass on the sagebrush flats, the sage grouse held community land. It was a stage used by all the members of their group. On it the males danced, displaying to the females their gorgeous feathers and the wondrous yellow air sacs on their necks.

On the day the chickaree babies were born, a male grouse ran across the dance floor as fast as he could go. His spiked tail was spread over his back. He dragged his wings to show off the beautiful white feathers on his rump. He lifted his neck feathers and the bright-yellow comb over his eyes. He was magnificent. Another male ran out to meet him. They vibrated their tails and drummed their quills like castanets. They closed their eyes and danced in a trance. Eventually the first male peeked at his rival, saw he still had his eyes closed, and sneaked away. The second male opened his eyes, saw he was foolishly alone and also ran. All this day and the next and the next for weeks, pairs of male grouse would meet on the community stage. The females would seem not to be watching the show-offs, but they would be.

Later, nests in the grasses with eight to twelve grouse eggs would attest to their interest.

The chickaree did not hear the sage grouse drum that morning. She was licking her babies to stimulate their hearts and lungs. When they were dry and breathing softly, she rested her head in her doorway and peered down at the river shore. The yellow holly grapes that grew close to the ground bloomed in the sunshine, and the golden flowers of the glacier lilies nodded in the wind. Their appearance meant the eggs of the bald eagles were about to hatch, and that the bighorn sheep were lambing.

The chickaree watched everything on the riverbank, for she was curious as well as noisy. She saw the magpie pick up a stick and show it to his mate, and she saw the mate lift her feathers in approval. Next, the magpie carried it to a cottonwood and put it in a tree crotch. It was the first of many sticks that would make up their nest.

While they worked, the chickaree dropped off

to sleep, curled around her babies.

"*Tshee, tsheee, tshee!*" She awoke in surprise. A tree swallow hovered at her door. Just back from the coast of the Gulf of Mexico, the bird was peeking into every hole in the forest to see if it would make a suitable nest.

"*TCHER-r-r,*" the chickaree screamed. The hole was definitely occupied. The swallow flew off.

A rustle sounded in the dry fir needles on the ground, and the chickaree looked down. Chewing at a biscuitroot plant was a field mouse. The chickaree ignored it, but the pine marten did not. He ran down from a tree, caught it, and ate it.

As the chickaree babies grew, the mother spent more time away from them. One morning she was stuffing seeds in her cheeks when she heard the *"killie killie"* of the kestrel, the smallest North American falcon. Only a week before, this colorful bird had returned from his wintering grounds in the south.

At first he had sat quietly on a tree stump, flying out to catch insects, then returning to look over his old home. In a few days he, too, felt the moon of April and began defending his property against neighboring kestrels. His nest would not be ready for another two weeks; his young would not hatch until June.

Farther up the riverbank, the red-tailed hawk warmed her eggs. Every three hours the female stood up on her stick nest and carefully turned them with her beak to keep the embryos from sticking to the shells. Then she sat down and relaxed into the broody silence of incubation, not hearing, not even seeing the lovely snowdrops and blue-eyed Marys bobbing all across the meadow before her.

The night that the full moon of April rose over the valley of the Bitterroot River, the mother chickaree squirmed and tossed. Her babies had grown so big, they were crowding her out of the hollow. She gave up and went to sleep in a crotch of the tree.

At dawn the babies awoke to hear their mother screaming at a coyote, then at her cousin, then at the magpie. Another April morning had begun. The mother nursed her youngsters and ran down the tree.

She did not stop until she reached the spruce cones she had stored in the water last fall. Pulling one out, she carried it to a stump and peeled the sheaths off the seeds and ate them. She ran up the hemlock where she had hidden dried huckleberries and hastily ate some of them. Then she checked her big storehouse, screamed to tell her cousin to stay away, and dashed off to eat buds in the cottonwood where the magpies had built their nest. The magpies dived and raged at her, for red squirrels are not above eating birds' eggs. She ducked their blows, then ran down the tree and into her forest.

Her day was just beginning. She scurried up a

lodgepole pine and looked in a hole where she had stored edible fungi. It was occupied by a black-backed woodpecker, who instantly flew at her. Jumping to a twig, she trapezed to a limb and crawled under a piece of hanging bark. Safe, she watched the woodpecker fly by.

The moon of the property owners' shenanigans kept the mother chickaree busy. One day she took her favorite highway through the trees to see if her cousin was at her stream. Suddenly, the trail ended in empty space. An aspen tree was missing. It had been cut down during the night by the beaver who slept in his lodge in the middle of his pond. The tree was now his property, not hers. When his mate, who was curled over their four newborn kits, had eaten her fill of the aspen bark, he would carry the tree to the dam and use it to raise the water level.

Finding no cousin, she circled the property. As she approached her storehouse, she heard chewing sounds. Someone was robbing her! She

dashed to the top of her food pile.

"TCHERR-r-r-r-rrrrrrrrrrrrrrrrrrrr," she screeched. A pack rat had a cone in her mouth. Hearing the angry chickaree, she ran ten yards to her own castle. Still carrying the cone, the rat slipped into a huge pile of sticks and grass and dropped her booty beside her most cherished possessions—a bottle top, a fish hook, and one shiny dime she had found by the river.

The pack rat cuddled around her fifteen-day-old young and went to sleep, her nose touching the cone that was now her property.

The chickaree was still scolding. When she became quiet, a thieving chickadee took a seed from her storehouse. Several young mice stuck their heads out of the tunnels they had made in it. Mice in a storehouse are a disaster. They would eat everything. She was torn. It was time to feed her babies, but she must save her property.

In frustration, she scolded for seven long minutes, then stopped. The forest was quiet, the

mice nowhere to be seen. Wearily she climbed up her tree toward her family. She had hardly gone halfway when she saw the magpie fly to her toadstool supply.

"TCHERRRRR." The chickaree was about to chase the bird when she heard her babies cry. The sound pulled her up the tree as if she were on a string. The moon of property owners' rights was also the moon of nurturing. She flicked her fuzzy tail and slipped into the hollow.

No sooner were her babies fed and cleaned than she was off again to check on her property. She must defend it. The lives of her offspring depended on it.

The magpie was now in the water, bathing at the edge of the river. He was nervously watching the sky. Suddenly he cried his alarm note and flew into the cottonwood.

The chickaree had learned that the birds, with their keen eyesight, saw enemies long before she did. She ran into a nearby hideout. A golden eagle came into view, his wings motionless as he rode the air current above the river. Here was a real enemy.

"*RRRRRRR!*" she warned. Every bird stopped what he was doing and sat perfectly still. Eagles see movement. Birds somehow know that if they do not move, eagles and other predators will not see them.

"*TCHERRrrrrrrrrrrrrrrr!*" The chickaree awoke the pine marten, who was sleeping at the top of a spruce tree.

The large slender marten, whose beautiful fur is known as sable, moved with sensuous grace. Chickarees were one of his favorite foods. He looked for the screamer, could not find her, and came down the tree like flowing water. He was met by another marten, who was passing through. The two males did not fight, for martens share their property with their own kind. The males have several mates, who raise the young by themselves in hollow logs and under fallen trees.

The woodpecker, who was drilling into a dead pine, saw the martens. *"Yk,"* he warned, and circled to the other side of the trunk so they could not see him. The chickaree heard this alarm and stayed where she was. The strange marten went up the mountain and the other ran to the marsh where the moose was browsing.

A hooded merganser saw the marten and swam into the grass, his black-and-white head now looking like sunshine and shadow. The marten did not see the bird.

The tree swallows saw the hunter and spread out over the river calling, *"CHI-veet,"* their alarm note.

Finding nothing to eat in the marsh, the marten circled back into the forest and climbed to a tree limb, still looking for the chickaree. Gathering his short, powerful legs under him, he leaped twenty feet to the limb of another tree. It was the chickaree's nursery tree. He climbed to the top and hid in its dense needles to wait for her.

The chickaree did not leave her hideout until she heard a pine siskin, a song sparrow, and finally a lazuli bunting sing. The caroling of the birds meant that there was no enemy to be seen. She ran out into the sunlight and back to her babies so swiftly that the dozing marten caught only a fleeting glimpse of her tail as she disappeared in her hole.

Safe, she listened to the male songbirds mark their property lines with songs. Birds tell other males of their kind not to trespass by singing. Melodies are their swords.

Along the river a western tanager had a problem. He had returned from the south to find a strange male on his last summer's property. This was not tolerable, because when his mate returned in a few days, she would take the male who owned the property as her partner, not him.

To prevent this, the tanager flew to a bush and faced his opponent. He lifted his feathers to make himself twice as big as he was. This frightened the rival, but he did not fly away. The tanager vibrated his wings. Finally he thrust out his beak, a sight as terrifying to a bird as that of someone pointing a gun toward a person.

The rival could bear it no longer. He gave up and flew down the river to find a piece of unoccupied land.

When he departed, the tanager threw back his head and warbled his property song over and over again.

The chickaree put her head out her doorway. She was ready to start off again. The marten tensed his muscles to spring. At that moment a baby fussed and the mother dropped out of sight to console it.

"TCHEEEEr," her cousin yelled. With that she dashed from her hollow and ran down the tree so fast, the marten did not have time to leap. However, he followed her to her storehouse.

In a rock crevice about two feet from the storehouse a rattlesnake was coiled. His heart-

shaped head swung slowly on his arched neck. The snake had just come out of his hibernation and was warming himself in the sunlight. He was still cold. He moved slowly, and the chickaree saw him.

"TCHERRRRRRRRRRR," she screamed. She jumped onto a low tree limb and rode with it down, then up, leaped to a higher limb and got away. The cousin saw the snake and froze in fright. The marten pounced on him.

That evening the chickaree did not hear her cousin. His poor property had forced him to trespass once too often.

Toward the end of April, the gray jay came to the river for a treat. Thousands of caterpillars were abroad. They rippled and humped as they climbed twigs and plants. The jay stabbed at one. The caterpillar reared its head and tail and curled into a circle. It looked so much like a bud that the bird did not recognize it as food. He hopped toward another caterpillar.

In the last days of April, the swallows were treated to a feast. The black flies hatched and flew over the river in dark clouds. All winter these insects had clung to submerged rocks in their larval stage. They looked like little palm trees, the "leaves" of which paddled food into their mouths. When the "palm trees" split open, the adults emerged inside bubbles of air. In these they floated to the surface, opened their new wings, and flew. Then the tree swallows feasted.

On the last day of the April moon, the jay called his mate to join him at the storehouse. The chickaree came on the run and found them eating her seeds.

This was too much to bear!

She climbed to her winter home, which was right above the storehouse, tidied it up, and rushed back to her hollow. Picking up a furry baby in her teeth, she carried it down the trunk, over the ground, and up to the winter nest. She laid it carefully inside, then went back for another

and another.

When all four were gathered in the home above the storehouse, the mother chickaree looked down contentedly. At last she could fulfill all the rites of the April moon with one scolding.

A good loud *TCHERRRRRRRRRR-r-r-r-r-r* from the top of the tree would protect both her young and her property. No one embodied the spirit of the April moon like the chickaree.

Bibliography

Brennan, Gale. *Earl, the Squirrel*. Chicago: Children's Press, 1980.

Carter, Anne. *Scurry's Treasure*. New York: Crown Publishers, 1987.

Coldrey, Jennifer. *The World of Squirrels*. Milwaukee, Wis.: Gareth Stevens, Inc., 1986.

Davis, Adrian. *Discovering Squirrels*. Mankato, Minn.: Crestwood House, 1983.

McConoughey, Jana. *The Squirrels*. Mankato, Minn.: Crestwood House, 1983.

Martin, Alexander C., Herbert Zim, and Arnold L. Nelson. *American Wildlife and Plants: A Guide to Wildlife Food Habits*. New York: Dover Publications, Inc., 1951.

Palmer, Ralph S. *The Mammal Guide*. Garden City, NY: Doubleday & Company, 1954.

St. Tamara. *Chickaree: A Red Squirrel*. Orlando, Fla.: Harcourt Brace Jovanovich, 1980.

Stanley, Colleen. *Tree Squirrels*. New York: Dodd, Mead, 1983.

Van Wormer, Joe. *Squirrels*. New York: E. P. Dutton, 1978.

Index